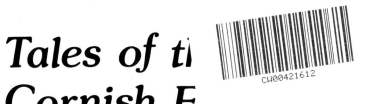

Tales of the Cornish Fishermen

CYRIL NOALL

TOR MARK PRESS · PENRYN

Second edition first published 1989
by Tor Mark Press, Islington Wharf,
Penryn, Cornwall TR10 8AT

© 1969, 1989 Tor Mark Press

ISBN 0-85025-314-4

Acknowledgements

The publishers are grateful to the Royal Institution of Cornwall for
permission to reproduce the photographs; they are also grateful to the
Curator of the Royal Institution, Roger Penhallurick, for his help with
picture research.

Printed in Great Britain by Century Litho (Truro) Ltd, Falmouth

OLD 'TEAK JOB' OF ST. IVES

Somewhere around the year 1848, Capt. William Stevens of St. Ives was in command of a sailing ship which while lying becalmed off the Moroccan coast was attacked by Moorish pirates. Capt. Stevens and his crew put up a desperate fight to prevent the ship from being taken; and while the master was firing the poop gun it burst, blowing off one of his hands. Despite this mishap they managed to drive off their attackers and make good their escape.

When he returned to England Capt. Stevens was fitted with a wooden arm, allegedly made of teak, whence arose the name by which he became generally known—"Teak Job", or "One-armed Job". Perhaps it would be more correct to say that this accounted for a part of his nickname; for it is not so clear how the "Job" originated. Indeed, "Job" proved to be a somewhat inapt cognomen for Capt. Stevens; for, unlike his Biblical namesake, he displayed little patience under misfortune, and became a morose, sullen-natured man, displaying a rather violent temper under the least provocation.

Yet, if he had not Job's patience, he more than made up for this deficiency by stoicism and fortitude. He continued to hold command of sailing vessels for many years longer, and then retired to live on his hard-earned savings at St. Ives.

There another disaster overtook him. He had unwisely invested his money in a shipping speculation, which failed in 1869; and Capt. Stevens now found himself reduced to earning his living by fishing. He did not join one of the regular St. Ives fishing boats' crews, however, but in his morose, independent way, preferred to go fishing alone in the Bay in a small boat, sculling the vessel with his one remaining arm.

In January 1873, E. D. Davenport, then occupier of Tregenna Castle, interested himself in the case of this courageous, though crusty, old seaman; and on his recommendation, "Teak Job" was elected a member of the Royal Alfred Aged Seamen's Institution—whereby he received a regular pension from that body.

The amount was, however, small, and Capt. Stevens was still

obliged to keep up with his fishing; but even in extreme old age maintained that spirit of enterprise and pluck which he had always displayed, as the following incident proved. In August 1879, a large quantity of gurnards, or "gurnets", as they were then called, was landed at St. Ives. The local market being soon glutted, these fish sold at a very low price. "Teak Job" accordingly purchased six score at sixpence a score, loaded the fish into his punt, and began to scull to Portreath, seven or eight miles miles away from St. Ives where he sold them at a remunerative price. A newspaper correspondent, referring to his feat, declared admiringly "that as he is 75 years of age, having one arm, and having to scull all the way, the performance must be considered marvellous, and certainly would tire many a younger man with the full complement of arms".

However, this writer, in his otherwise impeccable account of the affair, committed the grave and unforgivable mistake of referring to our hero by his nickname; and as, a result, was soundly rebuked in the following issue by the irate old sea-dog, who reminded him, in forceful language, that his correct name was Capt. William Stevens; that he had been a certified master mariner for thirty years.

A few years after this "Teak Job" fell on evil days. Most of his pension—£17 per annum—had for some time been spent on drink, and he was living in a most filthy and deplorable condition. In October 1884, he fell ill, and would have died alone in dirt and squalor if some neighbours, who heard his moans, had not come to his assistance. The Officer of Health was called in, and reported to the Overseers that the old man was in need of food and clothing, and had better be removed to the "Big House". Capt. Stevens, game to the last, gallantly resisted the officers when they came to take him away; but, alas, they proved to be tougher adversaries than the pirates he had fought forty years before; and so, in spite of his struggles, the courageous old sailor was unceremoniously "shanghaied" to Madron workhouse.

STEAM ON THE FISHING GROUNDS

Steamers began to make their appearance in Cornish waters as early as the 1820's; and stories are related from several parts of the coast of how local fishermen, on first sighting one of these vessels, put off in great concern to assist the "ship on fire". The obvious advantages which steam would have given to the drift fishermen of that period might lead one to suppose that experiments would have been quickly tried to discover how this new motive force could best be applied to fishing. Such, however, was not the case. The fishermen's traditional conservatism and a fear that the economic returns might not justify the capital outlay, meant that many years were to elapse before any steam drifter sailed out of a Cornish harbour. In 1876, however, Messrs. Harveys of Hayle, built a 43-ton steam-powered iron screw fishing boat for John Wedge, of St. Ives. Named *Patmos*, she was employed, when not fishing, as a packet steamer, mainly on the Hayle or St. Ives to Bristol run. A half-model of this interesting vessel is preserved in St. Ives Museum.

The earliest record that can be traced of the *Patmos* shows her acting as a cargo vessel. This describes how the steam lugger *Patmos*, of St. Ives, had left Hayle, in July 1876, for Rouen with sugar. In April of the following year we find her engaged in the fishing industry, for which she had really been designed. During the last week of that month, the St. Ives fleet had found the fishing very unproductive, owing to the weather. For some days they were prevented from going out by very high seas; whilst later a dead calm had exactly the same effect on all boats except the s.s. *Patmos*, which steamed merrily out of the harbour where all her companions lay helplessly becalmed. On this occasion she returned in triumph and landed 3,900 mackerel, which sold at a record price of 41s. per six score.

Later that year an attempt was made to use the *Patmos* to establish a regular sailing between Bristol and St. Ives for the conveyance of goods. The initial trip was made from St. Ives on the first Monday in October, leaving Bristol the following Friday on the return voyage. (It may be remarked that a steam packet service had been established between Hayle and Bristol as early as 1831 by the appropriately-named paddle steamer *Herald*, so that *Patmos* was hardly blazing a trail on this particular route.) The venture does not seem to have been successful, and next summer the little steam fishing boat was sent to try her luck on the Irish fishery. Luggers of the St. Ives fleet had been crossing the Irish Sea for this purpose for many years before this; and, no matter whether their catches were light or heavy, had always been civilly received by the natives of the "Emerald Isle". A different fate awaited the *Patmos*, however, both she and her crew being lucky to escape unharmed from the wrathful hands of the Irish fishermen!

She chose as her base the harbour of Kingstown (now Dun Laoghaire) south of Dublin. Trouble began when the steamer gave a repeat performance of the fine show she had put up when fishing at St. Ives during the spring of 1877. For during the whole time she was at Kingstown—this was the month of July—the weather remained calm, with the result that local boats were unable to land on average more than two catches each week, whilst the St. Ives lugger, through the advantage conferred by her engines, came in daily with good catches, which fetched excellent prices on the market.

This was rather more than Irish flesh and blood could stand; and the local trawlermen began to display an increasing animosity towards the "outsider". The climax came when an attempt was made to set fire to the St. Ives lugger. This, happily, was thwarted; but "the little steam-boat", says an account dated July 25th, "with her most inoffensive and respectable master, wisely left the place".

Despite her proven superiority as a fishing boat, the *Patmos* was an unprofitable speculation for her owners. An account of the vessel, published in a Cornish newspaper on October 24th 1878, states: "The large and excellent screw fishing craft *Patmos* was built by Messrs. Harvey & Co., of Hayle, about two years since at an expense of £1,300 for boat and engines. The venture in a 50 or 60 ton craft, and in the effect to utilise steam for fishing purposes, was a plucky thing, thought of by men who invested money which had been hard-earned abroad. Every effort was put forth to make her pay—in fishing, in trawling, in the North and Irish Channels, in the conveyance of potatoes from France, coal from Wales, merchandise from Bristol to Lelant, etc. Last week she was sold for £800 to a purchaser in London, who, it is understood, will employ her in the transport of goods on the River Thames, and she has sailed for her destination, calling at Plymouth on the way." According to Grahame Farr's *West Country Passenger Steamers*, she was soon after this sold again to new owners in South America, where her subsequent fate is unknown.

After this unfortunate experience, the St. Ives fishermen were reluctant to experiment further with steam. A second St. Ives steam fishing boat did not, therefore, make an appearance until 1885. This was the *Willie Warren*, S.S. 31, launched from a local yard. She differed from her predecessor in being fitted with paddles instead of a screw. Her dimensions were 57 ft. keel, and 17 ft. 3 ins. wide.

She was thus 3 to 4 ft. longer than any boat belonging to St. Ives, enabling her to carry about 20 nets more. The engine also worked the capstan, and the total cost came to about £1,000.

Great hopes were entertained for her success; but when she made a trial run across the Bay it was noticed that she lacked speed, her paddles seeming to be too small. The boat, indeed, suffered much from what might be termed "paddle trouble" during the early part of her career. Her crew experienced great difficulty in shipping and unshipping these cumbersome appendages, as circumstances required, so that she frequently lost the advantages they were supposed to confer, by this loss of time. Eventually, they were replaced by a propeller; and finally the engine was completely removed, the *Willie Warren* then becoming a sailing dandy.

This interesting boat was basically a mackerel lugger, but, like the *Patmos*, she also went into the freight trade, and during her later years became a sailing collier. Later again in 1901 she was once more fitted out as a steam fishing boat, and re-christened *Rebecca*. She was equipped for the drift fishery, the intention being also to use her for long-lining and trawling.

Three other steam vessels are known to have worked out of St. Ives in the early years of this century. They were the *Edgar*, the *Pioneer* and the *Adventure*, the last two being registered at Penzance, but working at St. Ives. All are said to have been very successful.

Ultimately, steam was replaced as a motive force by the altogether more convenient internal combustion engine, the first vessels at St. Ives to be so equipped (*c.* 1910) being the *Gleaner* (S.S. 123) and the *Golden Lily* (S.S. 14). Going back to the earlier days, it is interesting to see how the fishermen attempted to make use of the facilities of steam without actually having engines fitted to their boats. When the Cornwall Railway was opened in 1859, through rail communication between west Cornwall and the capital became possible, affording the fishermen a large and lucrative market. However, the fish trains had to be met at Penzance; and it often happened that the mackerel drifters found themselves becalmed at sea, laden with fish, and unable to make port in time to get them despatched. When eventually brought in, this "overday" fish was worth only about half of its original value, and usually had to be disposed of locally. Various expedients were tried to overcome the difficulty. The commonest remedy was to combine all their catches in one swift craft and despatch these united "takes" to shore; but even this failed in a dead calm. Then, in April 1869, the Mount's Bay men engaged a swift steamer, which waited on the fishing boats either at Scilly or another appointed rendezvous, and conveyed their fish as rapidly as possible to land. By this means, "there is no difficulty in placing on the Londoner's breakfast table fish which were disporting themselves a little more than 24 hours previously in the Atlantic, 40, 50 or 60 miles from the Land's End", as the *Cornish Telegraph* rather quaintly expressed it.

The vessel chosen for this work was the paddle steamer *Rover*, credited with a speed of twelve *miles* (*sic*) an hour. On April 27th, about forty boats handed her their small catches of from 50 to 200 fish, making 52 pads in all, caught two leagues S.W. of the Scilly Islands. (Pads were small oval baskets, each holding about sixty fish.) *Rover* conveyed them to Penzance in good time for the train, and on the London market they realised 30s. a hundred. Next day *Rover* took 210 pads. This new system had the further advantage of enabling the boats to remain continuously at sea, fishing all week without having to come in to land their catches.

There is some reason to think that *Rover* ran in conjunction with the Great Western Railway, so that the operation of this service served to augment the monopoly which they held in the west Cornwall fish trade. The rival London & South Western Railway Company cast envious eyes on this traffic, but were unable to obtain a share of it, as their lines did not extend far enough west to compete. However, in March 1871, it was announced that they had formed a venture, known as the West Cornwall Steam Fishing Company, with the object of using a vessel to penetrate into "enemy territory". A fast steamer would run, during the mackerel season, between St. Ives and Bideford, or Penzance and Exmouth, according to requirement. The fish would then be conveyed to Billingsgate market by special and other trains, "and *the whole line to London being under one management*" there would be no stoppage or delays. The L.S.W.R. contrasted this arrangement with the service provided by their rivals, alleging that "the greatest inconvenience has frequently been experienced, and heavy losses sustained, by consigners of fish . . . to the London markets, in consequence of there being but one route available for their conveyance".

FISHERMEN'S SUPERSTITIONS

As the pilchard season of 1843 drew to its close, the fishermen of St. Ives wore gloomy faces, as it had proved a very unsuccessful one, and many of the curing cellars remained largely empty. However, a local paper in November reported that "a superstitious notion prevails, that noises heard in the cooperage and in the fish cellars, are indicative of the arrival of the 'finny tribe', and as such sounds have lately been frequently heard and disturbed the people from their midnight slumbers, it is fully anticipated that the pilchards are on their march to this place!" The noises generally considered to be a good augury in this matter were two kinds—a squeaking sound emanating from the great blocks of pilchards already "in bulk" in the cellars; and the sound of pressing stones rolling about on the cellar floors.

The squeaking of the salted fish—usually referred to as "pilchards crying for more"—was explained as being due to the bursting of air bladders; and when many broke simultaneously, which, with hundreds of thousands piled in a mass, was not uncommon, the sound could be quite loud. The rolling of the pressing stones is less easy to account for in rational terms. These stones were circular granite beach boulders, each weighing about a hundredweight, and fitted with an iron hook. They were used to press oil and brine from the casks or hogsheads of salt pilchards being prepared for export. Robert Hunt recorded a story from St. Ives on this theme. A fishing family called Tregose, who lived over a fish cellar, found the pilchard season passing away without any signs of fish. One day, however, Ann Jenny Tregose and her daughter Janniper heard the press-stones "making a skimmage" in the cellar below; and when the boys came home that evening they also caught the sound of a heavy rolling of the stones. "It did not require much imagination to image these round granite pebbles sliding themselves down on the 'couse', or stone flooring, and dividing themselves up into sets, as if for a dance—a regular 'cows' courant', or game of romps." The old woman declared that this presaged "fish tomorrow". And she was right. Early next morning Tregose and his sons were on their stem; and shortly after dawn the cry of "Heva! Heva!" was heard from the hills; the seine was shot; and by night a large quantity of fish had been brought to the cellar.

All fishing is chancy; and pilchard seining particularly so, the appearance of the shoals being very erratic. Sometimes a sequence of years occurs without any being seen. This probably accounts for many of the various superstitions connected with this fish. A further example which may be given concerns the way in which pilchards should be eaten. They should always be eaten from the tail towards the head—which brings the fish to our shores, and secures good luck to the fishermen.

The dangers of his calling made the fisherman entertain some strange but understandable beliefs regarding death by drowning. He dreaded to walk at night along those parts of the shore where there had been wrecks. These places were supposed to be haunted by the souls of drowned sailors; and at certain times, particularly before storms, and at night, the "calling of the dead" could frequently be heard there. Many a fisherman declared he had heard the voices of dead sailors "hailing their own names". A story common around the Cornish coast tells how a voice from the sea was heard calling, "The hour is come, but not the man". After this had been thrice repeated, a black figure like a man appeared above the beach, paused momentarily, then rushed impetuously down into the sea, and was lost.

THE GREAT SUNDAY FISHING CONTROVERSY

The rise of the Puritan influence in England during the early seventeenth century was marked at St. Ives by the passing of a bye-law prohibiting Sunday fishing. Dated 1622, it reads: "It is agreed by generall consent, that hencfforth no owner of Boates or nettes shall dryve or sett their Nettes, or owner of Seanes rowe to Steame, the Sondaye nighte, or any tyme before Daye of that nighte; who shall herein transgresse, ech owner shall paye for his defaulte x^s & ech fisherman iij^s iiij^d to be levyed of ther goodes to the use of the parishe".

When Wesley came to St. Ives in the following century, his own brand of religious teaching—Methodism—included not a few of the precepts of the older Puritanism; and the great success which this movement obtained in Cornwall, and particularly at St. Ives, led to a strict maintenance of this Sunday fishing ban.

Religion was here strongly aided by superstition. A certain Mary Stevens, whose father had a large interest in the pilchard fishery, went down to the old fish cellars near the Market House one Saturday night, and urged the women "bulkers" to prolong their efforts into the early hours of Sunday morning. A large catch of pilchards had been landed, and much of this fish would be spoiled if left till Monday. The women agreed and Mary joined them in their labours until all the pilchards had been salted down. As Mary was on her way home, she noticed, when passing the open window of the old "George and Dragon" inn, the form of a man lying on the floor, upon which he appeared to be writing with his finger. It was pitch dark at the time, but she was clearly able to read what he had written by "a great light" which proceeded from his side, and the message was—as she might have guessed—"Remember the Sabbath Day, to keep it holy".

Despite such "warnings" as this, and their own religious scruples, the St. Ives fishermen were sometimes under great temptation to break this now time-honoured custom. It must, indeed, have been galling to have to stand idly by and watch a "lane" of pilchards passing through the Bay on a Sunday, following a week of unproductive fishing. Sometimes the temptation proved stronger than flesh and blood could stand. Thus, in August 1831, Capt. J. T. Short noted in his diary: "Some thousands of hogsheads of fish passed through the stems, in consequence of the seine concerns having agreed not to fish on a Sunday. The fish were passing from 11 a.m. until 7 p.m., when Mr. T. Tremearne put one of his boats to sea, and caught a fine shoal of 600 hogsheads."

Tremearne was the only man bold enough to flout tradition on this occasion; but when a large quantity of fish was discovered on another Sunday morning close to Carrack Gladden Point, "the finders immediately made hevva, but no notice was taken. Charles Tremearne then ran home to St. Ives, when all the boats were immediately manned; but . . . the fish had gone!"

When the Cornwall Railway was opened in 1859, it became possible to send mackerel—a highly perishable fish—to London very expeditiously from west Cornwall. Local fishermen were quick to take advantage of this new opportunity; and their colleagues from Lowestoft and other East Coast fishing ports quickly joined them in supplying this lucrative new market. These East Coast men —or "Yorkies", as they were usually dubbed—had, in the main, no tradition of Sabbath observance; and on their arrival in Cornwall, immediately began to catch and land mackerel on Sundays. This outraged the Cornish fishermen, both on religious grounds and for the more mercenary reason that this Sunday fish tended to choke the markets, leading to a fall in prices. As a result, much ill-feeling was generated, leading to discord and riots, with trouble simmering on until the end of the century.

In April 1860, an East Coast fishing boat came into St. Ives road-stead with about 1,000 mackerel caught on Saturday night, which were purchased by two strange buyers—the usual buyers, presumably, refusing to touch them for fear of antagonising the locals. A gig's crew of St. Ives fishermen refused to allow the fish to be landed, and after some altercation, threw the fish into the sea.

Far more serious trouble occurred in May 1876. One Monday morning several East Coast boats arrived with large catches caught the previous day, which were landed and offered for sale. A group of St. Ives fishermen made such a commotion around the auctioneer that the sale could not be proceeded with, and then a fearful disturbance began. The Mayor intervened to preserve the peace, but no sooner had he left the quay than the struggle recommenced. The "Yorkies" resolved to carry their fish to Hayle, and their boats proceeded to that port, but the St. Ives men attempted to prevent any carts proceeding to Hayle with the fish. A riot took place, hard blows being exchanged and stones thrown. An endeavour was made to set fire to the packing straw in the carts, but they succeeded in getting away to Hayle.

There was a repetition of these events the following year, when the St. Ives fishermen who "make their quays sacred against the foolish mackerel that get into the nets on Sundays" again prevented a landing of these fish. About fifty East Coast boats appeared in the offing on the morning of Monday April 9th, and a Shoreham craft sent her catch to harbour in a small boat, but was obliged by the mob to take them back again. The other boats then proceeded to Hayle.

The trouble now began to spread to other places. A correspondent at St. Mary's, Scilly, wrote on May 1 1877: "On Thursday night our usually little quiet town of St. Mary's was the scene of a disgraceful riot among the fishermen. Owing to the roughness of the weather a great many boats were in the harbour—amongst them a few East Country craft. During the evening a party of East Countrymen, about nine or ten in number, were in a room at the Atlantic hotel. Two or three West Countrymen got in with them, and a dispute arose which resulted in a free fight. The door being locked on the inside and cries of murder being heard, a number of West Countrymen broke in through the partition, and through the door and windows, and a terrible scene ensued.

"Glasses, pots, broken chairs, etc., were freely used. A report of what was going on reached the boats on the beach and brought a good many more men on the scene. The policeman and constable, too, were quickly on the spot and managed to get the two parties separated. The West Countrymen were now outside, to the number of nearly 200 men, and in a very excited state, vowing that they would pull the house down to get at those inside.

"The magistrates were called out about half past eleven p.m.; and, it having become known that the Riot Act was about to be read, and that the Coastguards, under Mr. Bulley, were at hand fully armed, the crowd quickly dispersed and went to their boats.

"The East Countrymen then came out and claimed magisterial protection. Mr. Hall told them—three of them being captains and one owner of their respective boats—that they must consent to go up in the prison; else their safety could not be secured. To this course they unwillingly agreed, and were put in the lock-up in the Garrison till next day, when all being quiet, they went to their boats.

"During the riot the hooting and yelling by the excited crowd was fearful. One East Countryman, who tried to make his escape, but was seen and chased by at least 100 men, reached the pier first, jumped into the water, and swam out of reach, pursued by the most frightful yells from his disappointed and furious followers. Another was caught on the sand and kicked and beaten very badly . . ."

Whilst this was going on at Scilly, the St. Ives men inserted a claim in their conditions of sale that any purchaser of fish caught on Saturday or Sunday nights and landed at St. Ives "or elsewhere" should be disqualified from bidding at their sales. The effect of this continued opposition was to drive the East Coast boats from St. Ives to Newlyn, which thus became the principal fish market in the west, a large and important fishery harbour to accommodate the increasing trade being subsequently provided there.

There had never, however, been complete unanimity among the St. Ives men on this Sunday fishing question; and during the winter of 1887 a violent dispute broke out between two local factions. The practice had been established that, during the autumn herring fishery no fish should be caught between twelve (midnight) on Saturdays and one a.m. on Monday mornings, thus preserving the inviolability of the Sabbath. However, St. Ives being a tidal harbour, the larger fishing boats began to find themselves at a serious disadvantage as compared with the small gigs; for whereas the latter could put to sea at any state of the tide, the former had to wait for high water before they could go afloat. As a result, the larger boats were frequently unable to do any fishing at all on Monday mornings, for the catching of herring can only be done during the hours of darkness.

This naturally led to friction between the two classes of fishermen; and those with larger boats soon started putting to sea late on Sunday evening so as not to be left high and dry by the ebbing tide. To begin with, these boats waited religiously until one o'clock before casting their nets overboard; but soon this rule was relaxed, and they began to fish openly in the late hours of Sunday evening. Not to be outdone, the gigs followed their example; so that it was not long before fishing was started by some boats as early as five p.m. on Sundays—just as on an ordinary week-day, in fact. All this aroused the indignation of the "Sunday keepers"—still the overwhelming majority among the fishermen—and after a meeting had been held to consider the matter, the town crier was sent round to

announce that it had been decided no boats should put to sea on Saturday nights or Sunday mornings.

Five boats nevertheless decided to defy this ban and shoot their nets on Saturday evening. They put to sea; and a large crowd gathered on the beach awaiting their return. As soon as the herring boats came within hailing distance, they were told that they would not be allowed to land their fish, but must throw their catches overboard. The boats dumped their fish at sea; nor did anyone venture out on the following Monday morning.

The local dissidents apparently made an effort to break the ban a year or two later; and in the autumn of 1890 another meeting of fishermen agreed not to go to sea from Saturday morning till Monday evening. Almost at once, two or three boats broke the arrangement, and went fishing for herrings on Monday morning; but the few fish they landed could not be disposed of by auction, there being no salesmen and no buyers, and the herring had to be hawked round the town, without success.

Meanwhile, the dispute between the East Coast and Cornish fishermen was steadily moving towards a climax. After being driven from St. Ives, the Eastern men continued to land their Sunday-caught fish at Newlyn, where for some time this practice was tolerated, though hardly approved of by the local men. Eventually, however, the glutting of the markets by the East Coast boats caused such injury to the Mount's Bay fishermen that opinion began to harden against them. It was pointed out that the East Coast boats had been obliged to discontinue Sunday fishing along the Irish coast, and it was felt that they should be made to observe the local custom of Cornwall in this respect also. The Eastern men, however, refused to come to any agreement.

Failing to persuade them by remonstrance and negotiations, the Mount's Bay men, supported by their brethren of Porthleven, in May 1896, resorted to the extreme step of destroying the fish which the Lowestoft boats had brought into harbour together with the cargoes of three others lying just outside. Fully 100,000 mackerel were thus disposed of. Great excitement prevailed and police reinforcements were sent for. A Lowestoft man who complained about the morning's occurrences was set upon by a dozen local fishermen, who beat him severely. Penzance Borough Police were kept in readiness and a large number of special constables sworn in.

During the afternoon the Newlyners paid a visit to Penzance

hoping to seize further cargoes of fish for destruction. An East Coast boat had been seen making for Penzance, and the crowd hoped to prevent her making a landing. But the object of the boat was only to obtain ice to enable them to carry the fish to Plymouth, and they had succeeded in getting one block on board before the mob arrived. Seeing that the Newlyn men had manned their gigs to board the boat, the drifter at once set sail and put off to sea again. The crowd vented their fury on a fishbuyer's office, which was dragged by ropes into the harbour.

On Tuesday morning six more Lowestoft boats came into Newlyn, and their cargoes were immediately pitched overboard. In the afternoon the crowd attempted to reach Penzance quay, but after a conflict with the police were driven back.

Realising the seriousness of the position, the authorities telegraphed for gunboats and troops. A special train conveyed about 350 men of the Royal Berkshire Regiment to Penzance in the evening, and the detachment was marched to Newlyn, headed by half-a-dozen magistrates. They were received with jeers and hooting, and a crowd that showed no disposition to disperse. The troops took possession of the southern pier, and cleared it of all except East Countrymen, who were ordered to leave at once with their boats, which they did amid jeers and howls, just as the *Ferret* torpedo boat destroyer steamed into Mount's Bay off the harbour.

Leaving a small number of soldiers to guard the pier approach, a strong body of troops and police, again headed by the magistrates, marched through the main streets of the town to the Eastern Pier. Though the crowd made way for them, they howled and yelled like madmen, and hurled all kinds of missiles at the representatives of law and order, repeatedly shouting that they could take care of their own harbour, and would allow no interference. Three Lowestoft boats were making for Newlyn, but the soldiers warned them off by firing several volleys into the water.

In consequence of the continued serious rioting, H.M.S. *Curlew* and H.M.S. *Traveller*, each with an armed party of seamen on board, were despatched to Mount's Bay to join H.M.S. *Ferret*. Meanwhile, news of the disturbance reached a large contingent of the St. Ives fishing fleet, then at Scilly. According to local tradition, they at once set sail for Newlyn, with pennants flying, like an Armada, to show their support for the Mount's Bay men, and put into Newlyn on Tuesday evening.

By Wednesday, Newlyn was much quieter, but the fishermen refused to put to sea, and affirmed their determination to put a stop to Sunday fishing. The military and police remained on duty and during the evening, a large party of youths from Penzance (where some sympathy was felt for the Lowestoft men) accompanied by some "Yorkies", marched to Newlyn. Stones were thrown, and windows smashed. The military were called in, who cleared the Newlyn-Penzance road of intruders as far back as the old Penzance borough boundary. A picket was placed along the road, and at the western end of Penzance promenade a cordon of military and police was drawn to prevent a recurrence of this incident. The Lowestoft and Yarmouth fishermen were now accommodated in Penzance dock, and the Town Council, at a special meeting, decided to offer them every facility for disposing of their fish during the remainder of the season. Another warship—the *Leda*—had now joined those already anchored in the bay, although no men had been landed from them. Meanwhile, the Home Office refused to receive a deputation of Newlyn fishermen, but agreed to receive a statement from them.

On Thursday, a meeting of fishermen held at the pier entrance appointed a deputation to meet representatives of the Lowestoft Boatowners' Association at Penzance, but the latter refused any overtures until £800 damages had been paid. The Fishermen's Committee then drew up their statement to the Home Secretary, which read, in part: "From our great-grandfathers' days down to the present it has been the custom of our port to refrain from fishing on the Saturday night and Sunday night, so that we might have a clear market on Tuesday morning, and have a chance of keeping the Sabbath as well. Lowestoft and Yarmouth men take advantage of this, contrary to the rules or customs of the port, fish on the Saturday nights and Sunday nights, and after being out several nights, make it a point of coming to market on Monday morning with their fish in a decomposed condition, swamp the market with these rotten fish, and so destroy the week's market. St. Ives men have succeeded in stopping them from coming to their market with Sunday fish for years; Irishmen, Manxmen, and Scotchmen have succeeded in doing the same—(we are speaking of drift-fishing now)—and we Cornish Sabbath-loving people only ask them to do the same. We have tried by petitions, and by appeal to local gentlemen to get our grievance redressed, but we could not succeed in bringing the matter before the public until now. True, some of the young lads have gone further than the law would allow; and we have repeatedly asked them to desist from doing anything against the law in the hearing of the military and the police, as they can testify, and we have done no damage to life or property, except in throwing away the Sunday fish as a protest. There are Lowestoft men while we write throwing their fish overboard to show their sympathy with us, and we have a great many Lowestoft men with us. It comes to this, that if Lowestoft men are allowed to persist in doing this, the £100,000 worth of fishing property, owned mostly by the men by whom the boats are manned, is not worth today as many pence, and our wives and children must starve."

In the next few days the position at Newlyn eased. The St. Ives and Porthleven fleets left port, and the majority of the Berkshire Regiment were withdrawn to Devonport, leaving a company of a hundred men to assist the large force of police still retained there. A deputation of Cornish fishermen, representing Newlyn, Mouse-hole and Porthleven, went to London, where one of them made serious—and probably well-justified—charges of over-fishing against the East Coast trawlers, some of which shot a line of nets 4-5 miles long, seven days a week, during the spawning season, as a result of which mackerel were getting scarce.

During the following September about thirty Cornish fishing boats returning from the North Sea fishery were obliged to beat about off Lowestoft owing to adverse winds and four of them, all from St. Ives, put into the harbour there. They were subjected to a certain amount of jeering; and the following morning when putting to sea two of them were stoned as they passed the pierhead from the herring basin. The men took cover behind the bulwarks, and the skippers, who were steering, behind the sails to avoid injury. The fishing boats made for H.M.S. *Renard*, a fishery protection vessel anchored in the roads, and lodged a complaint, which was investigated. The only St. Ives boat remaining in the basin was the *Gyles*, No. 441, which had grounded on the bar when endeavouring to enter Southwold harbour the previous night. Some beach men floated her off and took her to Lowestoft, claiming £50 for their services. As the amount was disputed, she was arrested. The skipper (James S. Gyles) on learning that the other boats had been stoned, and the crew threatened, appealed to the coastguard for protection. The police were instructed to keep watch upon the craft, which

was moored in the middle of the basin and only accessible by boat.

On January 2nd 1897, a meeting of St. Ives fishermen, boat-owners and salesmen, passed resolutions affirming their stand on the Sunday fishing principle. Reference was also made to a forthcoming conference to settle the Newlyn dispute. On January 8th, the Lowestoft and Yarmouth boatowners, salesmen and skippers met at the Suffolk Arms in Lowestoft, to consider the future working of the westward voyage. It was agreed that their boats should work from Plymouth as long as possible, and then go to Penzance, only running into Newlyn when compelled by unfavourable weather.

A meeting of the Newlyn men took place later in the month to consider a suggestion from the Board of Trade, that a compromise settlement of the Sunday fishing dispute should be adopted, by which East Countrymen should refrain from fishing on Saturday nights. At this meeting there were considerable disturbances, many men shouting that they would have two nights or none, and fight to the bitter end; but after speeches by delegates to the London conference and from Mr. Bolitho, M.P., it was resolved by a large majority to accept the suggestion.

However, echoes of the dispute continued to resound for some time after. On the morning of Tuesday, April 6th, the East Coast lugger *Boy Jack* put into St. Ives harbour to sell her fish, having left Penzance the previous Sunday morning. The St. Ives men at once attached a rope to the lugger and hauled her out of the harbour. She sailed out into the Bay, and disappeared around the land, a strong gale blowing at the time. This rough weather had kept the St. Ives fleet in harbour, and a large number of fishermen had assembled on the pier. "Considering the rough usage some of our boats experienced when away last year, we cannot help remarking that the St. Ives fishermen exercised a considerable amount of forbearance", wrote a local commentator. That same evening another Lowestoft fishing boat put into St. Ives, the *Toiler of the Deep*, a "Sunday keeper". She had left Penzance on Monday morning and shot the same night, the wind blowing a strong gale from S.S.E. The nets became fearfully entangled when the wind suddenly flew round to N.N.W., and they were parted by a passing steamer and lost. Sailing about for an hour, they managed to pick up their 140 nets again, and after experiencing terrible weather managed to reach St. Ives. In this case, the locals did all they could to help the stranger. They moored the boat safely, and at once began to clear the nets, so that what in the ordinary way would have taken the crew several days to do, was completed the same night.

As recently as August 1929, a riot occurred at St. Ives on this Sunday observance question. A pleasure-boat operator announced he was going to run a speed boat from St. Ives on Sundays; but a mob of fishermen assembled and threw him back into the harbour when he attempted to land. They afterwards marched along the Wharf Road and smashed all the slot machines in sight. Even today, the effects of this prolonged and bitter controversy are still very much in evidence. St. Ives harbour remains religiously closed on Sundays; whilst the fact that it is—for fishing purposes—virtually a ghost port, though Newlyn, the premier fishing station of the west, continues so prosperous, is directly attributable to the same cause. Originally, the East Coasters preferred St. Ives, which had direct rail communication with London, a facility lacking at Newlyn. However, local hostility drove them from St. Ives to that port, where a magnificent harbour was built for the use of both Mount's Bay and visiting boats. Despite the antagonism shown them there at the time of the Riots, Newlyn's position had become unchallengeable, and has remained so ever since.

FISHING BOAT DISASTERS

Seventy or eighty years ago Cornwall's ports were crowded with hundreds of fishing boats of different types, nearly all of which relied on sail for their motive power. Remembering that fishing was a year-round occupation; that some of the best grounds lay in the vicinity of dangerous submerged reefs; and that the Cornish coastline is one of the most treacherous in the world, it might be assumed that casualties among the fishing fleets would be high, and the loss of life equally so.

Disasters, did, indeed occur; one has but to enter the little medieval chapel of St. Leonard, on Smeaton's Pier at St. Ives, and read the list of names on the fishermen's memorial there, covering the period 1833 to 1940, to realise how grim a toll was exacted by the sea in this one port alone. However, severe as these losses were, the surprising thing is that they were not much greater. Consider the case of an entire fleet of pilchard or mackerel boats caught at sea in a sudden storm; one might expect literally dozens of them to be wrecked, and their crews drowned. Yet this never happened. Two or three, at the most, might suffer this fate; the rest, somehow, would struggle to harbour, or find the shelter of a lee shore. It was not good fortune which saved them, but the superb seamanship of their crews, and the incomparable knowledge which these men possessed of local tides and currents.

One of the worst fishing boat disasters at St. Ives occurred on November 22nd 1872. During the afternoon the fleet of mackerel and pilchard boats were on their respective fishing grounds, when, towards nightfall, the wind freshened to a gale. The pilchard boats in the Bay made at once for the pier, where they arrived at nine o'clock, but the mackerel boats, being farther off, and the wind against them from the southward had to beat hard to get in. Most gained the shelter of the pier by 3 a.m. on the 23rd but eight boats were still missing, and great anxiety prevailed for them. At daybreak, one of them, the *J.P.H.*, belonging to Capt. John P. Hodge, was sighted two miles off the Head, her anchor down and her mizzenmast gone. The large fishing lugger *Ebenezer* was at once manned and eventually took off the five men on board. During the afternoon, the *Boomerang*, living up to her name, returned with 6,000 fish, her crew being completely exhausted from their ordeal.

Later, it was learned that the lugger *Daniel* had arrived at St. Agnes; whilst two more—the *New Susan* and the *St. Peter*, after losing all their canvas, brought up within Towan Head during the afternoon and were subsequently warped into Newquay. The *Ellen Noall* reached safety at Ilfracombe after riding for 24 hours to a raft.

Two boats still remained unaccounted for and eventually news reached St. Ives that a 30-ft. fishing boat, together with nets and fish enclosed, had been washed ashore at Stanbury Mouth, near Bude. The bows and stern were gone, and but one mast remained. She bore the number "S.S. 411"—this being the number of the *Mystery*, owned by Mr. John Paynter. She carried a crew of five, among them, three sons of the owner. Of the other boat—the *Captain Peter*—nothing was ever heard or found. Altogether, ten men had been lost, six of whom left wives and families.

When fishing at night, or in fog, boats ran a serious risk of being run down by passing merchant vessels. A sad example of this occurred in March 1871. As the Lowestoft boat *Happy Return* came in from the fishing grounds at daybreak she sighted wreckage about seven miles S.W. of Porthleven. She found that a fishing boat had been completely cut in two, so that she could sail between the two parts, amid a tangle of gear that held the halves together. The punt was got out, and with a kedge anchor the Lowestoft men raised bow and stern of the wreck. On the first was painted "No. 335"; on the other "Desire, of Porthleven". They picked up the hatches and brought them to Penzance. The Mousehole boat *Rodney* later reported that she had been fishing near the *Desire* that night. At about eleven o'clock a large ship sailing west towards Land's End carried away part of the *Rodney's* nets. It was observed there was great confusion on board this ship and it was thought this was the vessel that had run down the *Desire*. Two Porthleven boats, the *Wonder* and *Mary Jane*, put out to sea and brought the two sections of the wrecked boat into Porthleven harbour. In the bow part, a watch was found hanging in the usual position on deck, stopped at 4.45, and in the sleeping berths were some of the crew's clothes, proving that the men could not have been drowned in their berths. The *Desire's* small boat was missing. Altogether there had been eight persons on board: the owner and master John Strick; his two sons; a grandson; a nephew; two other men; and a boy, who was on his first fishing trip.

The *Desire* met her fate in the darkness of night, unseen by anyone on land or even by friendly fishing boats nearby. Far different was it with the Mousehole fishing boat *Jane* which was lost whilst running for shelter to Penzance during the great Mount's Bay storm on October 7 1880. She was smashed to pieces and her crew drowned amidst the tremendous seas in full view of the spectators on shore. The gale began at midnight on the 6th from the west, but later swung round to the east, and blew its hardest from S.S.E. Great damage was caused to the sea front at Penzance, comparable to that of the great storm of 1962. Many vessels broke adrift in the harbour, driving ashore, and others being involved in collisions after they had parted their moorings, great damage being caused despite heroic efforts by the pilots and "hobblers" to secure them.

The *Jane* had put in at Falmouth on the 6th for a while, and then set sail for Penzance. As she rounded the Lizard she was caught in the storm and had to make her way through mountainous waves and a screaming gale. However, the watchers on Penzance pier were not unduly worried for her safety, for she was a sturdy craft, typical of the well-designed Mount's Bay luggers. She appeared in sight shortly before seven o'clock with only a small sail up, and actually came within fifty or a hundred yards of the Extension lighthouse without mishap. Near this place, however, the conditions were particularly dangerous. The usual rush of big waves was sometimes overtopped by a fiercer roller still, its white-tipped crest stretching from just off the pier down to the Ryeman pole. A cross-sea from west to east would then rush along the trough between two of these tremendous billows; and it was the double twist given by these which caused the boat to be swamped.

The *Jane* rose on the crest of the biggest wave that had been seen that morning. It seemed to lift her quarter and swing her bows round towards the Mount. Not only was she thus nearly broadside on, but one of the treacherous cross-seas caught her, and, as if she was in a whirlpool, her bows tilted to the S.E., and she fell over—deck to the full southern sea and gale. Her fate was now sealed, and in five minutes she had broken in pieces. Two of her crew disappeared almost at once, and of the remaining five, three quickly succumbed to the merciless fury of the elements. The two who were left put up a desperate struggle for life, clinging to pieces of wreckage, and trying to fight their way through the maelstrom of waters to the pier such a short distance away. The quay pilots summoned both the lifeboat and rocket apparatus in an effort to save them; but though the fishermen managed to keep afloat for fifteen minutes in those raging seas, clinging desperately to their supports, they were at last overwhelmed and drowned. Only five minutes later the rocket apparatus reached the pier, just too late to be of service.

Many of the fishing boats lying at their moorings also became casualties during this storm. At Newlyn eight or nine were sent to the bottom, stranded on the shore, or wrecked on the rocks. Eleven boats were destroyed at Mousehole. The loss of nets and foot-lines was also very great, for the storm broke so suddenly there was no time to take in those left on the walls to dry. About a hundred St. Ives, Newlyn and Mousehole fishing craft were moored in Penzance harbour; several of these sank, others received serious damage. Altogether, about thirty Mount's Bay fishing craft were lost in this terrible storm.

The loss of fishing gear which sometimes occurs on such occasions can represent a major disaster for the fishermen. This gear represents a great deal of hard-earned invested capital; without it, he cannot continue fishing, and his livelihood is gone. A major catastrophe, involving the loss of nearly a thousand nets, struck the St. Ives fishing fleet in April 1882. On the night of the 27th about fifty boats were on the fishing ground, where they had just shot their nets, when, almost without warning, a N.W. hurricane sprang up and carried away almost every net. The cost of a mackerel net at that time was reckoned at £3, whilst the estimated value of lost fish varied from £5 to £20 per boat. But, worse than this, the boats were now rendered idle right in the midst of the mackerel season. The total loss was conservatively placed at £5,000. "To properly realise what this means", wrote a correspondent at the time, "it must be borne in mind that many of the owners of the nets are men who live almost from hand to mouth, and who have not in hand the price of a single net. Many I spoke to are men with a wife and four or five helpless children depending upon them for the bare necessaries of life. The glistening tear and the doleful accents of the poor fellows as they recounted their distressed position were in themselves painful testimony to the anguish they felt. A more melancholy sight than forty or fifty boats on the beach with not a yard of twine or a mesh amongst them can scarcely be conceived."

The men, nevertheless, were lucky to escape with their boats and lives. Many boats were obliged to beat about for two days before returning to harbour, only to be overtaken by another gale when in sight of St. Ives. The Island and cliffs were thronged with the wives and children of the fishermen, shrieking with fear lest their loved ones should be lost while entering port. The wind blew with hurricane force from N.W., and the men, almost exhausted by exposure and overwork, had a hard struggle to win through to safety. Two boats, the *Theodore* and *Express*, could not fetch St. Ives, but were driven before the gale into Hayle, whilst the *Hopeful* was nearly dashed on the rocks. Eventually the *Covent Garden* lifeboat was sent out with fresh crews to replace the exhausted fishermen, and by this means the boats were all eventually brought to safety. Two St. Ives boats were, however, lost in this terrible storm. The *Grace Darling*, skippered by Capt. Curnow, after riding to anchor in Mother Ivey's Bay, drifted in near the cliff; but the seven men on board were rescued by rocket lines fired by the Coastguard. Scarcely had the last man been drawn to land than the boat parted her cable, drove ashore and in a few minutes became a total wreck. The second St. Ives boat was lost when, in company with several others, she was endeavouring to reach safety at Newquay. Failing to round the Head, she went ashore on Holywell Beach, the crew fortunately reaching land in safety, apparently using their punt.

THE VOYAGE OF THE *MYSTERY*

Much has been written on the emigration of Cornish miners during the last century to the United States and other mining settlements abroad; it seems, however, less widely recognised that many other classes of workers—fishermen, agricultural labourers, tradesmen— also joined the great exodus overseas. This group of emigrants did not, in the main, join the colonies of miners, but dispersed among the general population of their adopted countries, and so have been lost to view to Cornish historians.

Many interesting tales, nonetheless, could be told of this latter group of expatriates. One of the best of them concerns the voyage made by seven Cornish fishermen from Penzance to Melbourne in a 16-ton fishing boat, called the *Mystery*, during 1854-5. It was a journey made without any of the publicity attending the recent adventures of round-the-world yachtsmen, in an ordinary fishing boat having neither radio nor any of the sophisticated navigational aids available today. One must regard it as a truly heroic exploit;

yet the men who took part in the voyage would probably have been surprised to hear it described in those terms.

It so happens that one of them—P. C. Mathews—wrote a tantalisingly brief account of their odyssey in 1874 in order to correct a garbled version of it which a Penzance newspaper gave in an obituary notice of another member of the crew, Charles Boase, of Newlyn. Plainly written as the story is, it requires the exercise of no great imagination to appreciate the sterling qualities of the men and the boat which made this remarkable voyage:

"We left Mount's Bay on the morning of the 18th of November 1854, with a crew of seven men—Richard Nicholls, Job Kelynack, Richard Badcock, William Badcock, Lewis Lewis, Charles Boase, and myself. Our cargo consisted principally of provisions and water. On March 14th 1855, we cast anchor in Hobson's Bay, Melbourne, thus accomplishing the voyage in 115 days, including seven days' stoppage at the Cape of Good Hope, where we put in for a supply of water. We were eight days from England to Madeira, and on the 35th day out we made the Island of Trinidad. On the morning of the 17th of January 1855, we arrived at the Cape of Good Hope, being 59 days out. On January 24th, at 6 p.m., we got underway from Cape Town and proceeded on our voyage with H.M. mails on board. Nothing interfered with our progress until February 18th, in lat. 40.5 S., long. 82.5 E., where we encountered a very heavy gale, which necessitated our riding to a raft for nine or ten hours. Riding to a raft is a system adopted for safety. Ships heave-to under such circumstances. On February 23rd, another heavy gale visited us in lat. 39.57 S., long. 98 E. We again rode to a raft for four or five hours. On the 5th March we met with another very heavy gale in lat. 40 S., long. 129.19 E., which compelled us to ride to a raft for 12 to 14 hours. The weather was pretty favourable after that date until we got to our destination."

The *Mystery* was 33 ft. long and 11 ft. 6 in. beam. It is said that before setting out on their voyage the fishermen decked her, as she had previously been an open boat. On arriving at Melbourne, they sold her, and found various kinds of employment for themselves. Of the seven, five eventually returned to their native home. Of the two who remained in that country, Lewis Lewis died in Castlemaine, whilst Mathews settled in Melbourne. Nicholls, the captain, after making many other voyages, and on the point of starting from London on another, was knocked down by a dray and killed.

"OLD DUTCHY"

During the latter half of the last century large numbers of fishing boats left Cornwall in June and July for the North Sea herring season, returning to their home ports again in September. Every fisherman would bring back with him some presents for his family and friends. One of the most popular for the children was a stick or two of Scarborough rock; whilst for their elders there were often sets of earthenware "Whitby pans"—shallow dishes used for domestic purposes—and similar articles.

In the early 1880's, however, many of the men started to bring home expensive bottles of perfume and packets of good quality tobacco, which were duly distributed among their delighted kinsfolk. As fishermen were a somewhat impecunious lot, much surprise was occasioned at their apparent sudden access of wealth. The explanation was, however, a simple one. The North Sea fishing grounds had been invaded by a number of Dutch "coopers"—

floating shops—from whom uncustomed goods could be purchased at only a fraction of the prices ashore. These transactions took place on the high seas, where the Customs authorities were powerless to interfere; although it was, of course, an offence to bring such goods ashore. However, the fishermen had few scruples on this point, smuggling having never been regarded as a very serious sin in Cornwall.

For a time everything went well with these "Free Traders". They and their friends maintained a discreet silence, and the local Customs officers seemed to have no suspicion of what was going on.

However, the amount of tobacco illicitly landed at St. Ives eventually became so great that the shopkeepers began to notice a marked decline in their sale of it; and one of them, incensed by his serious loss in trade, informed the authorities what was going on.

This was during the summer of 1884. The fishing fleet was then still away; and the Chief Customs Officer of St. Ives and the Coast-guards made preparations to "rummage" them on their return. The first boat to arrive—the *Charles*—came in on a Monday morning in early September, a few days ahead of the main part of the fleet. She was promptly boarded by a commissioned boatman of the Coast-guard, who discovered two half-pounds of tobacco on board; and the boat's owner was duly brought before the magistrates, charged with smuggling. The bench inflicted a fine of £1 0s. 6d. and 5s. 6d. costs, with the alternative of one month's imprisonment; but the money was immediately paid.

The case caused consternation at St. Ives, as it was the first of its kind ever brought against a local fisherman. Anxiety now began to be felt by the relatives of the hundreds of men who at that very moment were sailing home from the North. There seemed, at first, no means of warning them of the hot reception prepared against their return. Then someone proposed sending a small boat out in the offing to inform the fishermen, as they approached, of the danger.

At first this measure proved highly effective. As the boats came in, one by one, during the rest of that week, they were warned by the small boat to dispose of any contraband on board before entering harbour—presumably by throwing it overboard. By Friday September 12, however, the boats were arriving in greater numbers; and probably because of this, two of them—the *Majestic* and *Matilda*—failed to receive warning of the rummage that was proceeding in the harbour. Accordingly, when these boats came in, the Coastguards, in searching them, "drew blood". On board the *Majestic* they discovered three bottles of perfume belonging to three young members of the crew. No attempt had been made to conceal the articles. After the Coastguard had impounded the bottles the fishermen were allowed to go about their business, but later in the day they were told to come to the police station.

Word quickly spread of what was happening; and a crowd of sympathisers soon gathered round the doors of the old Town Hall in the Market Place (where the police court and "lock-up" were situated); and whenever a Coastguard appeared, he was greeted with groans and jeers. The three men were remanded until Wednesday; but it was then learned that one of the *Matilda's* crew had been taken to the Custom House on an accusation of attempting to smuggle tobacco and cigars. After considerable delay he, too, was brought to the Town Hall by P.C. James Bennetts, St. Ives' famous "only policeman" in the Victorian era, followed by hundreds of people, who made the streets ring with cheers for the smugglers and groans for the obnoxious Coastguards. This young fisherman was, however, also soon released, like the others, on remand.

Towards evening the main body of the North Sea fleet began to appear outside the harbour. During that night and the following morning no less than forty vessels arrived. It was a thrilling spectacle to see these sturdy sailing craft come home again to St. Ives after several months' absence; and on this occasion a new note of drama was added by the events which had occurred earlier that day. A large crowd had assembled on the quays and landing places; and as one after another of the fishing boats ran in, they were greeted with loud cheers. Owing to the arrival of so many vessels in so short a time, the small staff of Coastguards were unable to make an effective search and in fact may also well have been intimidated by the large and hostile crowd. At all events, no further discoveries of contraband were made.

The trial of the accused fishermen took place on September 17th. It was argued by the defending solicitor that excisable goods on coasting vessels must be declared at the Custom House within 24 hours of arrival in port. The *Majestic*, however, had been searched as soon as she grounded, without giving the crew any opportunity of declaring the perfume. The perfume, moreover, had not been concealed. The charge brought against them would consequently seem to be without foundation. The magistrate's verdict was that he could find no evidence of an attempt to land the goods illegally, and the cases would therefore be dismissed, was received by an outburst of applause from members of the public who had packed the small courtroom, all friends of the fishermen.

When silence was at last restored, the Mayor appealed for order, and complained in strong terms at the absence of the other magistrates who should have been present to assist in trying the cases. These gentlemen had doubtless kept away to avoid the odium that would have fallen on them had they been obliged to convict, for public sympathy was entirely with the accused.

The case of the member of the *Matilda's* crew charged with attempting to land illegally a quantity of Cavendish tobacco and cigars was then proceeded with. The magistrates here could not agree on a verdict. The Mayor gave his view that as the goods had not been removed from the fishing boat into the punt, the defendant could not be convicted of illegal landing. His colleague did not concur with this opinion; so the Magistrates' Clerk entered a record in the Magistrates' book: "The Bench not agreeing, the case is virtually dismissed, without prejudice to either party".

The St. Ives fishermen had thus come off very well in their "brush" with the Customs, their only casualty being the conviction of the unfortunate skipper of the *Charles*. There can be no doubt that the Customs men in their zeal to check the landing of contraband, had acted with undue precipitancy, bringing a series of charges which could not be substantiated. By using a little more cunning they might have been more successful; but even so, the strong community spirit which prevailed among the fishermen must have made his task very difficult.

The effect of these cases was to make the fishermen more circumspect in their choice of presents when returning from the North Sea voyage. Some years later, however, a new kind of temptation was placed in their way. One of the coopers, registered in Holland, and popularly known as "Old Dutchy", began to anchor outside St. Ives Bay, where she was visited by local fishermen, who made extensive purchases of duty-free rum and tobacco from her stores which they brought ashore concealed amongst their gear. These transactions usually took place at night; and for some time the Customs officers, though highly suspicious, could obtain no definite proof as to what was going on.

At last, in desperation, the Customs authorities decided to send spies among the fishermen to find out what what was happening. These newcomers were very friendly, liberal with their tobacco, and always ready to stand drinks. As a result, they were soon in possession of all the information required.

A raid was thereupon carried out on the houses of those known to be trafficking in the smuggled goods, and a large quantity of tobacco came to light, hidden away in cellars, lofts, outhouses, and other unlikely places. At one house, in the Warren, some tobacco had been concealed in a bedroom. When the revenue men arrived and announced they were going to search the premises, the lady of the house said she had no objections, but would they allow her to tidy the bedroom first, as the bed was not made? They graciously consented, whereupon she rushed upstairs and hurled the tobacco through the window on to the rocks below. When the officers had left, after finding nothing, the tobacco was retrieved and secreted in a much safer hiding place until the affair had blown over.

"Old Dutchy" also spent some time off the Scilly Isles selling goods to the fishing boats. The lugger *Hugh Bourne* boarded the Dutchman there on one occasion and purchased considerable quantities of roll tobacco and perfume. These goods were stowed away in a secret locker aboard the fishing vessel. This locker could be opened without keys or handles, the method of doing so being known only to one or two members of the crew. On reaching St. Ives, the *Hugh Bourne* was boarded by the St. Ives Customs officer, who made a thorough search, but failed to find any contraband. Coming on deck, he told the skipper that he knew perfectly well there were smuggled goods aboard, as the *Hugh Bourne* had been reported to him as having been in communication with "Old Dutchy" off Scilly. The skipper retorted that if there was any tobacco on board, there should be no great difficulty in finding it. The officer then resumed his search, but without result. Later, the articles of contraband were taken from the locker and brought ashore at Porthgwidden, concealed in baskets of mackerel. The mackerel were duly taken down over Dick's Hill to the harbour and sold in the usual way; but how the perfume and tobacco were disposed of, is best left to the imagination.

As the "searchers" were carrying out their raid, word quickly spread through the town, and those who had sufficient warning hid their tobacco in the safest places they could think of. Some relatives of the author are reputed to have concealed a large quantity of contraband in the roof of Zion (Countess of Huntingdon's) Chapel, in Fore Street. Large amounts of tobacco were buried on the Island, where some of it might still be found, if one only knew the right places to dig!

However, despite these stratagems, the authorities succeeded in making a good many seizures. Not wishing to be too severe on the fishermen, however, they permitted them to escape prosecution by paying duty on all tobacco found in their possession. Two inn-keepers, also implicated in the affair, were later brought to trial. The ramifications of the smuggling were so widespread, and feeling in the town running so high, that the Government deemed it prudent to station a gunboat at St. Ives at the time of the trial. Accordingly, H.M.S. *Renard* was sent round from Holyhead and dropped anchor in the Bay the day before it was held, Commander Paton, the chief officer, subsequently attending the court proceedings in person. However, this precaution proved unnecessary, as everything passed off in an orderly fashion.

The first case heard was that brought against the proprietress of the ancient "Sloop Inn", on the Wharf. In the face of the evidence arrayed against her in court, in the form of seized tobacco, the lady had no option but to plead guilty to both counts. The solicitor for the Customs thereupon consented to drop the second charge, for

which the penalty was £20, if she consented to pay treble the duty and value on the tobacco involved in the other summons, to compromise the matter.

The landlord of the "Sloop's" neighbour, the "White Hart", was then charged with having on April 29 1898—the day of the raid—on his premises "1 lb. 8 ozs. of Cavendish tobacco, with which had been mixed ten per cent of liquorice, and which was not enclosed in a label, contrary to the Manufactured Tobacco Act, 1863". This defendant also pleaded guilty, saying the tobacco was bought for his own use, and not for sale.

There have been no prosecutions for smuggling at St. Ives since that time, the authorities' show of force having finally convinced the fishermen that the game had become too dangerous to play.

CORNISH FISHERMEN AT WAR

Several incidents involving Cornish fishermen and German submarines operating near the coastline occurred during the First World War. One of the most interesting concerned the St. Ives drifter *Mary Ann*. Owned and skippered by Capt. Matthew Stevens, she had been newly fitted out in 1914 for the mackerel season with a brand-new engine at a cost of over £400, and carried over eighty mackerel nets. She was actually the first boat to commence the mackerel drift fishery that year from St. Ives.

At sunset, eighteen miles from land, the seven-man crew were preparing to cast their train of nets when to their surprise a German U-boat surfaced near them. Its captain ordered them to get into their jolly-boat at which Stevens protested saying, "Surely you don't mean to harm a defenceless crew like we are?" Replying in very good English, the U-boat Captain said he could not help it, as his orders were "to sink everything at sight".

The fishermen then got into their punt, and watched while the Germans sent the *Mary Ann* to the bottom. The U-boat then submerged, leaving the St. Ives men alone on a wide sea. Though not far from shore, their position, in such a small boat, was not an enviable one. After three and a half hours their distress signals were seen by a merchant steamer, which rescued them. The water was by then up to the gunwales of their punt.

On returning to St. Ives, Captain Stevens commissioned the building of a new drifter to replace the lost *Mary Ann*. When she was eventually ready for launching, a name for her had to be decided on. The one chosen was *Sheerness*, in memory of the steamer of that name which had saved him and his crew after the U-boat attack. The *Sheerness* later became one of the best-known members of the St. Ives fishing fleet and is still (1969) in existence, but as a pleasure craft at an East Coast port.

During the spring of 1915 another Cornish mackerel boat, the *Children's Friend*, of Mousehole, was fired on by a German submarine, but, unlike the *Mary Ann*, managed to escape her pursuer. She was about five miles off the Scillies, with about 700 mackerel on board, when, without any warning, a shell was fired over the boat, falling into the sea only a short distance away. The *Children's Friend* was proceeding under sail at the time, making about six or seven knots in a favourable breeze. The look-out on deck shouted a warning to his companions below to come on deck. The engine was started and run at full speed, thereby increasing their rate of progress to about ten knots. Two more shots were fired by the U-boat, but both fortunately missed. As they approached St. Mary's the fishermen were thankful to see the submarine making off, and they reached the harbour there in safety.

THE *ROSEBUD'S* VOYAGE TO LONDON

The inter-war years marked a period of decline and change for all Cornwall's fishing communities. As the fleets dwindled in size, many fishermen were obliged to look for alternative forms of employment. And not only was their livelihood threatened; their homes were in danger as well. Up-country strangers were buying up their picturesque cottage homes at enhanced prices, driving the occupants to new housing estates remote from the harbours where they worked. This process of uprooting fishing families from the homes where they had lived for generations was accelerated by a Governmental policy of "slum clearance", under which many ancient buildings and streets were ruthlessly swept away.

Complaints and protests were made about these changes; but only in one instance was any positive action taken by the affected people to safeguard their homes. This took place at Newlyn, in October 1937, and led to the local fishing boat *Rosebud* sailing to London in an effort to persuade Parliament to reprieve a number of cottages scheduled for demolition. A clearance order, made by Penzance Town Council, covered much of the older part of Newlyn adjoining the quay; and the fishermen who lived there were to be re-

housed on a new estate at Gwavas, inconveniently situated on the hillside well above the harbour.

A petition, signed by over a thousand people from Newlyn and the adjoining fishing village of Mousehole, read: "We, the undersigned inhabitants of Newlyn and district, wish to protest respectfully and strongly against the wholesale destruction of our village. This ruthless appropriation of private property involved in most cases the loss of a lifetime's savings and the means of livelihood. We claim that no such drastic action has been permitted in any other part of the country. We earnestly beg your very serious consideration of this disaster with which we are confronted."

The epic voyage of the *Rosebud* to London had about it something of the flavour of a religious crusade—doubtless reflecting the fact that the nine members of her crew were all Methodists. Before her departure, a service of intercession was held in the old Primitive chapel in Boase street; and when she left harbour the villagers lined the quayside and sang "Fight the good fight".

Rosebud sailed early on the morning of October 20th in brilliant autumnal sunshine, to the cheers of a huge crowd of well-wishers. Their voyage along the English Channel and up the Thames to Westminster Pier—a distance of 460 miles—was accomplished uneventfully. Their visit had been preceded by a tremendous build-up of publicity, however; and on stepping ashore they found themselves the centre of attention. Capt. Alec Beechman, M.P. for St. Ives, greeted them on the pier steps, and they then made their way to interview Sir Kingsley Wood at the Ministry of Health, wearing their navy blue fishermen's jerseys. Sir Kingsley gave the *Rosebud's* crew a very friendly reception, and promised to study their petition, to see what could be done.

Rosebud herself, gaily decked with flags, proved a great attraction to the Londoners, many of whom paid sixpence to come on board and make a wish on a bottle of water from the celebrated well at Madron. The crew also had with them a bottle of Jordan water to bring good luck to themselves. If public sympathy and support could have ensured success for the crusade, then Skipper Cecil Richards and his men would have achieved everything they set out to do. Thousands of well-wishers expressed their whole-hearted support for Newlyn's people's fight to save their homes, and many wished to sign the petition, but this could not be allowed.

On the same day that *Rosebud* reached London, a party of women from Newlyn left Penzance with a petition to the Queen. Among them were wives of the *Rosebud's* crew and the skipper's daughter, Hilda, who represented the youth of the village. Their arrival attracted almost as much publicity in the capital as that of the fishing boat herself.

Rosebud took her departure from the Thames on the morning of October 27th and reached Newlyn early on the 30th. Her crew, naturally enough, were regarded as the heroes of the hour; but when the Minister's decision regarding the petition was announced, it became clear that they had gained, at best, only a partial victory. Of 157 properties included in the clearance orders, 23 were to be totally reprieved; 54 would be purchased at their market value; whilst of the remainder payments would be made to 17 as well maintained houses. One block of property only would be demolished, this being considered beyond repair. Where new buildings were to be erected, the old facades would be kept, to retain the character of the area.

So, it was this compromise scheme which was actually carried into effect, instead of the original plan of wholesale destruction. A number of old cottages were retained, to the delight of their anxious occupants and the satisfaction of both artists and holidaymakers. But more were swept away, in the name of progress, and Newlyn, like many another old Cornish town and village, has been aesthetically impoverished by the change. Admittedly, the problem of making old but picturesque properties conform with modern living standards is a difficult one; but this brutal expedient of demolition represented a confession of total failure by the planners.

Rosebud (PZ 87) subsequently changed both her ownership and name, being re-christened *Cynthia-Yvonne*. But it is under her original name that she passes into history as the Cornish fishing boat that sailed to London to save the homes of the Newlyn fisherfolk.